Want to know EVERYTHING there is to know about

JAMES ARTHUR?

Then step this way...

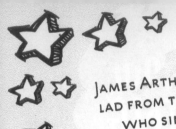

James Arthur is the gritty, tattooed lad from the North East of England who sings from the heart. The boy with soul, and bags of urban cool who took on 10,000 other applicants in The X Factor 2012 –

and came out on top!

People said that singers like James don't usually enter **The X Factor** – and they certainly don't win. But James's performances just kept getting better and better. He tackled songs from **ABBA** to **Adele** and gave them his trademark 'James Arthur twist' – making them cool, modern, edgy and **very, very catchy**. His performances wowed the judges, the studio audiences and – most importantly – the viewing public and the voters at home.

Nearly **13 million viewers** watched James and fellow contestant **Jahmene Douglas** battle it out for the top spot on Sunday 9 December 2012. Not only did James pull it off, his winner's single **Impossible** sold a whopping **1,300,000** copies in the UK, spending 18 weeks in the charts, and two weeks at Number One. James went from zero to hero in just three months!

You are obviously already a big fan of Britain's new singing superstar - but how much do you really know about James Arthur?

Do you know...

* Where he was born?
* What bands he has sung in?
* What colour his eyes are?

This book tells you **everything** you need to know – from who his best mate at school was, the songs he sung on the **X Factor Live Shows**, and even what other stars think of James. In fact, you're just a few pages away from becoming one of James's most knowledgeable fans – with our help!

And what can you do with this knowledge? We suggest stuffing all your **new-found facts** into a big James Arthur-sized bag and pulling them out one by one to amaze and amuse your friends. (Or you can just stuff the bag under your bed and let the cat sleep on it...)

WANT TO KNOW
YOUR IDOL?

Then grab a pen and some paper and start here!

Full name: James Andrew Arthur

DATE OF BIRTH: 2 MARCH 1988
BIRTHPLACE: REDCAR, MIDDLESBROUGH
LIVES: SALTBURN-BY-THE-SEA
HEIGHT: 191CM (6 FEET, 3 INCHES)
EYE COLOUR: BLUE
HAIR COLOUR: BROWN
FIRST SCHOOL: INGS FARM PRIMARY
  SCHOOL IN REDCAR
BEST FRIEND AT SCHOOL: MICHAEL DAWSON
FAVOURITE FOOD: NANDOS
TWITTER NAME: @JAMESARTHUR23
INSTAGRAM: ARTHUR2323

FAMILY

PARENTS: NEIL AND SHIRLEY
BROTHERS AND SISTERS: NEIL, SIAN, CHARLOTTE, JASMINE, NEVE.

JAMES ANDREW ARTHUR WAS BORN ON 2 MARCH 1988 IN REDCAR, MIDDLESBROUGH IN THE NORTH EAST OF ENGLAND. JAMES ADMITS TO DRIVING HIS MUM AND DAD MAD WHEN HE WAS LITTLE, AND WAS 'ALWAYS MESSING ABOUT AND GETTING TOLD OFF'.

Tut!

But as well as getting up to mischief, James **LOVED TO SING.** Aged just six, he remembers warbling along to anything and everything that his mum put on the CD player. Everyone told him he was very good at singing even at such a young age!

We don't doubt it.

As well as encouragement from his mum and dad, James inherited their broad musical tastes. Mum was listening to **Michael Jackson** and **David Bowie**, meanwhile Dad was headbanging to **Black Sabbath**, **AC/DC** and **Led Zeppelin**.

Oof, turn it down, Dad!

MEET THE FAMILY

DAD, Neil

Neil Arthur is a delivery driver. He
remembers James winning a kids'
karaoke contest when he was about 13.
'James sang Bryan Adams **(Everything
I Do) I Do For You** – the whole place
just went silent.'

MUM, Shirley

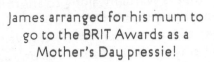

James arranged for his mum to
go to the BRIT Awards as a
Mother's Day pressie!

OLDER BROTHER, Neil

James seems to share his love for
music with brother Neil, who
plays the drums and used to be in
a band when he was younger.

OLDER SISTER, Sian

Sian works for a media and marketing company in North East England, and was a big help rallying votes for James during **The X Factor Live Shows**. She's one of his biggest fans!

YOUNGER SISTER, Charlotte

Charlotte Arthur is an art and design photography student at Middlesbrough College. 'One year James hadn't got me a birthday present, so he rang up and asked to be put on loudspeaker. He had written a song for me and performed it down the phone.' Nice one, James.

STEPSISTERS, Jasmine and Neve

Little sister Neve joined James on set during the filming of **The X Factor**. James often talked about how much he missed his family, and couldn't wait to give them all a hug!

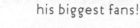

James admits he wasn't a star pupil at school...

But he did really enjoy English – particularly creative writing. He loved making up stories and exercising his imagination. Great practice for songwriting, we reckon!

James is not so keen on Maths. 'I only like doing things I can do really well in,' he admits.

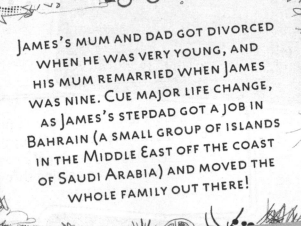

JAMES'S MUM AND DAD GOT DIVORCED WHEN HE WAS VERY YOUNG, AND HIS MUM REMARRIED WHEN JAMES WAS NINE. CUE MAJOR LIFE CHANGE, AS JAMES'S STEPDAD GOT A JOB IN BAHRAIN (A SMALL GROUP OF ISLANDS IN THE MIDDLE EAST OFF THE COAST OF SAUDI ARABIA) AND MOVED THE WHOLE FAMILY OUT THERE!

All of a sudden, James and his family were living the high life. They lived in a mansion with a **swimming pool**! James loved his new school, and the fact he was mixing with children from lots of **different cultures**. It was in Bahrain that he made his first public appearance – in a school musical playing an undertaker!

But that wasn't the end of the story...

Unfortunately, after a few years, James's mum and stepdad divorced, and the family moved back to Redcar, UK.

James admits to finding it hard to fit back into his old life. He became disruptive at school - playing up just to get people's attention, and often getting thrown out of classes.

His behaviour got so bad that he ended up in foster care for his last year at school. James was embarrassed about being in care, and didn't even tell his friends. If they were walking home from school he would pretend he was going to a relative's house instead of going home.

But on the positive side, this was when James began learning the guitar, and taking his music more seriously. He got a second-hand guitar for Christmas and loved it! He taught himself how to play, and started writing songs...

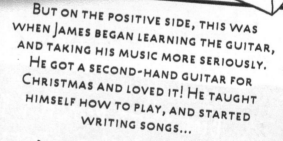

...about girls and broken hearts!

James with his
✗Factor mentor,
Nicole Scherzinger.

15

James Andrew Arthur

Scramble up the letters and what do you get?

A warmth jar ensured

A wanderer jams thru'

A rajah murders newt

Warheads ramjet run

Warranted jam usher

Rearward humans jet

Warmhearted jar sun

Hardwares jam tuner

Try it with your name. What do you get?

JAMES WAS BORN ON **2 MARCH**, WHICH MAKES HIM A **PISCES**. ASTROLOGERS RECKON THAT MAKES HIM LOVING, SENSITIVE, LOYAL, SPIRITUAL, IDEALISTIC AND DEVOTED. GOOD AT WRITING, ACTING, POETRY AND – YES – MUSIC!

Astrologers suggest that Pisceans get on best with people born in the star signs of **Cancer**, **Scorpio**, **Taurus** and **Capricorn**. They get on less well with those born under the star signs: **Aries**, **Gemini** and **Sagittarius**.

what star sign are YOU?

James shares a star sign with singers **Justin Bieber**, **Rihanna**, **Will.i.am**, and **Adam Levine** from **Maroon 5**. He's also counts actors **Daniel Craig** (aka **James Bond**) as a fellow Piscean, as well as Apple founder **Steve Jobs** and all-round super boffin **Albert Einstein**!

ACCORDING TO THE CHINESE ZODIAC, JAMES WAS BORN IN **THE YEAR OF THE DRAGON.**

Not only does that sound pretty cool, it IS pretty cool. It is the sign that all Chinese Emperors used as their official birthday. They would also cover their robes with embroidered images of the fiery beasts!

Find your date of birth here to discover which sign of the Chinese zodiac you are:

8 February 1997 — 27 January 1998	Ox
28 January 1998 — 15 February 1999	Tiger
16 February 1999 — 4 February 2000	Rabbit
5 February 2000 — 23 January 2001	Dragon
24 January 2001 — 11 February 2002	Snake
12 February 2002 — 31 January 2003	Horse
1 February 2003 — 21 January 2004	Goat
22 January 2004 — 8 February 2005	Monkey
9 February 2005 — 28 January 2006	Rooster

After his GCSEs, James took a music course at his local college. He learned some **MUSIC THEORY** (that's songwriting and other stuff), plus was able to practice playing live with other students on the course.

Unfortunately, he often couldn't afford the travel costs to get to college, so he **dropped out** after a year. But it didn't stop James pursuing his dream of becoming **a proper musician**! He kept on songwriting and singing, and formed his first band with a few other local boys. They were called...

...Traceless!

But sadly they soon disappeared without a trace!

IN FACT, THE MOST EXCITING THING TO HAPPEN TO **TRACELESS** WAS PLAYING AT A VENUE THAT THE **ARCTIC MONKEYS** HAD PLAYED THE WEEK BEFORE. THEY ALSO ONCE SUPPORTED A BAND CALLED **BROMHEADS JACKET**.

Bromheads who?

(Bromheads Jacket are a garage band from Sheffield, UK)

When **Traceless** split up, James played with a few different bands, including Moonlight Drive, Cue the Drama, Heroes and Hand Grenades (who later changed their name to Save Arcade), The Emerald Sky and The James Arthur Band. Phew. He was busy!

THE ODD ONE OUT!

WITHOUT PEEKING, CAN YOU
REMEMBER WHICH ONE OF
THESE BANDS JAMES
DID NOT APPEAR IN:

Traceless

Save
Arcade

Heroes and
Hand Grenades

Moonlight
Drive

Cue The
Drama

The James
Arthur Band

The
Emerald Sky

Home Alone

22

⭐ ⭐ ⭐ STRANGE SONG TITLES ⭐ ⭐ ⭐

PRE-**X FACTOR**, JAMES RECORDED
SEVERAL SONGS WITH THE BANDS HE
WORKED WITH (SEE OPPOSITE PAGE).
BUT WHICH SONGS ARE REAL, AND
WHICH HAVE WE SNEAKILY MADE UP?

Fatal Mistake

Misguided Beard

Drastic Action

Hole in My Heart

Tonight We
Dine in Hades

Superhero

Lost a Fiver

Juliet is Not Dead

Skinny Chimp

Hero Worship

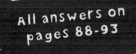

All answers on
pages 88-93

But singing and performing in bands is what James loved!

The problem was, he wasn't making much money out of it. On a good month, he might play a few gigs at local pubs, **singing covers** (versions of other artists' songs) and earn £150 per night. That would be his rent and bills sorted.

other months, he wasn't so lucky...

James slept on friends' floors, and even spent some nights **sleeping rough**, but he tried to stay focused on his music. He got friendly with the owner of a **local recording studio**, and recorded some CDs to sell at his gigs. He even recorded a couple of singles, but nothing ever came of it.

Friends kept texting James saying, '**The X Factor** is coming. If you don't enter, we're going to fall out with you.' Eventually, he thought, 'What have I got to lose?'

James's journey to pop superstardom had begun...

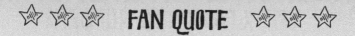

FAN QUOTE

OMG JAMES ILY SO MUCH I SUPPORTED YOU SINCE THE BEGINNING OF X FACTOR AND I WAS SO HAPPY WHEN YOU WON AND THEN I SAW YOU ON THE X FACTOR TOUR AND YOU WERE AMAZING. WOW XXXXXXXXX XXXXXXXXX

Morgan, 12

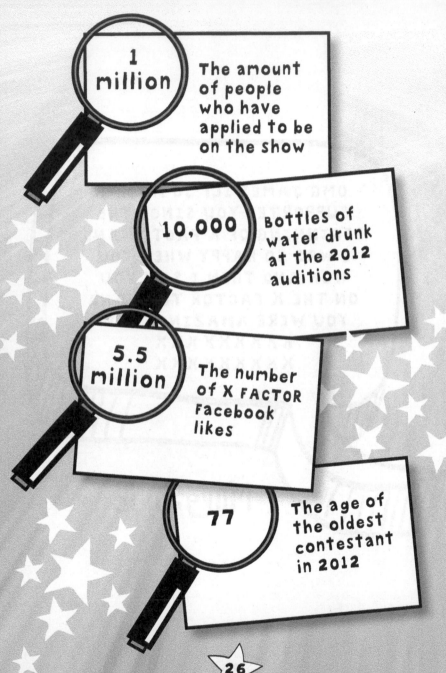

1 million
The amount of people who have applied to be on the show

10,000
Bottles of water drunk at the 2012 auditions

5.5 million
The number of X FACTOR Facebook likes

77
The age of the oldest contestant in 2012

900 The number of auditionees Dermot O'Leary spoke to in 2012

We Found Love 2012 contestants' most popular song choice

187,000 The number of copies IMPOSSIBLE sold in first 24 hours of release - making it the fastest-selling track of 2012, and the fastest-selling X FACTOR single ever!

13 million The number of viewers who watched THE X FACTOR final 2012

James really didn't think he was pop star material. He knew – or at least believed – he was a good singer, **BUT WAS HE COOL ENOUGH…?**

Even on the day of the **AUDITION** in Middlesbrough, James still wasn't sure the contest was for him. He certainly didn't feel like a **POP STAR,** nor did he think he really looked like one!

BUT HE WAS DETERMINED TO GIVE IT A GO, SO HE BORROWED £10 FROM HIS MUM FOR THE TRAIN JOURNEY, PUT ON HIS TRUSTY JEANS AND JUMPER, GRABBED HIS ACOUSTIC GUITAR, AND SET OFF FOR THE AUDITION.

The first auditions are in front of the **producers**, not the real judges. Still nerve-shredding, but at least you're not singing in front of **four famous faces** and a huge studio audience! James picked the **Alicia Keys** song **Fallin'** and one of his own songs called **Habit**, and did well enough to make it through to the **live auditions in Newcastle**.

Now it was time to get properly nervous!

JAMES HAD A FEW BUTTERFLIES BEFORE STEPPING ON TO THE STAGE AT THE NEWCASTLE LIVE AUDITIONS. HE WAS USED TO PERFORMING IN FRONT OF A FEW DOZEN PEOPLE – NOT THOUSANDS!

But he told himself to concentrate and not get star struck. Cheeky James even performed a fab version of Tulisa's song, **Young**.

'I decided that I could tell my [own] story through [the song]. When I was singing... I felt like I was asking for forgiveness from anyone I'd ever hurt.'

The audience cheered, Tulisa told James it was the best audition of the day, and Gary Barlow told him he wouldn't change one single thing about him.

Then it was time for the verdict...

After four 'yes' votes from the judges, James was in tears. He went off stage and hugged his mum and dad, who were both there to support him.

'I thought, "Brilliant, I might actually get somewhere with this music stuff now."'

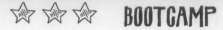 
For X FACTOR hopefuls, Bootcamp can be the start of a new life...

...or a big fat kick in the teeth!

James knew that only **six** boys from the hundreds at Bootcamp would be chosen for **Judges' Houses**, so his chances were tiny! It made him want to try harder than ever to **impress the judges**.

James's first task was to sing with his roommates from THE X FACTOR hotel – with only one of them making it through! James's name was called, but he had no time to celebrate before he was singing again – this time solo. He sang Take That's A MILLION LOVE SONGS in front of Gary Barlow, who wrote the song!

'When the audience and judges stood up and applauded at the end it felt totally unbelievable.'

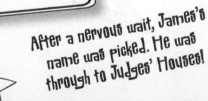
After a nervous wait, James's name was picked. He was through to Judges' Houses!

JAMES ARTHUR you smashed it every week. You always came out and gave your best and you deserved to win. Well done mate... at least we have some new talent out there, and talent that can actually sing...

whoop whoop!

Sethi, 13

Match the judge to the house!

During every series of **The X Factor**, the contestants jet off to some amazing locations for the **Judges' Houses** round of the competition. Can you match the judge to the location?

Louis Walsh
2012

Nicole Scherzinger
2012

Tulisa
2012

Gary Barlow
2012

Louis Walsh
2011

Tulisa
2011

Gary Barlow
2011

Kelly Rowland
2011

Louis Walsh
2010

Dannii Minogue
2010

Cheryl Cole
2010

Simon Cowell
2010

Dubai

Barcelona

Las Vegas

London

Los Angeles

Spain

Miami

Shannon, Republic of Ireland

St Lucia

Los Angeles

Greece

Melbourne

All answers on pages 88-93

JAMES HAD A TASK ON HIS HANDS ON
HIS TRIP TO DUBAI. IT WAS MAKING
HIMSELF UNDERSTOOD BY NEW **X FACTOR**
MENTOR AND HAWAIIAN-BORN SINGING
SUPERSTAR **NICOLE SCHERZINGER**.

She couldn't understand his accent!

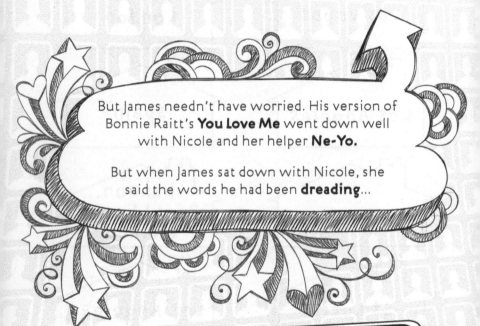

But James needn't have worried. His version of
Bonnie Raitt's **You Love Me** went down well
with Nicole and her helper **Ne-Yo**.

But when James sat down with Nicole, she
said the words he had been **dreading**...

'James, it's not good news...'
Hang on a minute, that's not right..

'...It's amazing news!'

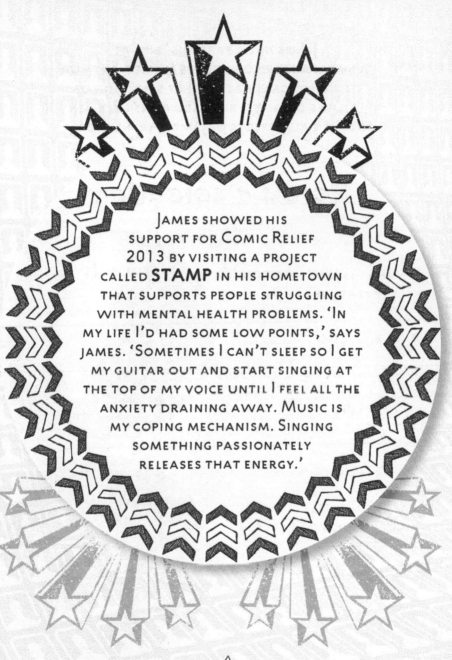

James showed his support for Comic Relief 2013 by visiting a project called **STAMP** in his hometown that supports people struggling with mental health problems. 'In my life I'd had some low points,' says James. 'Sometimes I can't sleep so I get my guitar out and start singing at the top of my voice until I feel all the anxiety draining away. Music is my coping mechanism. Singing something passionately releases that energy.'

WHAT THE FANS THINK

JAMES HAS A FAB FANS' SITE AT
WWW.FANPOP.COM/CLUBS/JAMES-ARTHUR
THAT NOT ONLY HAS A GREAT SELECTION OF
PICTURES OF JAMES, BUT ALSO RUNS EXCELLENT
POLLS ON ALL ASPECTS OF JAMES ARTHUR-DOM!

Here's a selection:

WHAT IS JAMES ARTHUR'S BEST FEATURE?

- His eyes **57%**
- His songwriting/singing **29%**
- Other **14%**

DO YOU PREFER IT WHEN JAMES SINGS OR RAPS?

- Sings **100%**
- Raps **0%** (oops!)

38

When did you first start to like James?

- First audition **67%**
- Judges' Houses **33%**

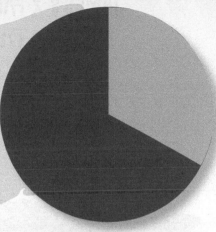

Who should James sing a duet with?

- Gary Barlow **55%**
- Professor Green **33%**
- Bruno Mars **12%**

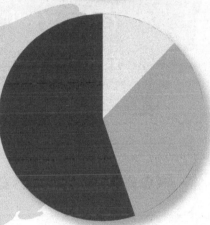

Who did you think would win The X Factor 2012?

- James **90%**
- Jahmene **10%**

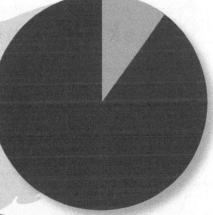

For the 10 weeks of **The X Factor Live Shows**, our idol did a 'James Arthur version' of an existing song to match each week's theme.

Can you match the week to the songs?

Week 1 Theme: Heroes

Week 2 Theme: Love and heartbreak

Week 3 Theme: Club Classics

40

Week 4 Theme:	Hallowe'en

Week 5 Theme:	Number Ones

Song choices

No More Drama

Don't Speak

Sexy and I Know It

Sweet Dreams
(Are Made of This)

Stronger

41

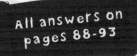
All answers on
pages 88-93

NONE OF THE PERFORMERS KNEW WHAT TO EXPECT WHEN THEY STEPPED ONTO **THE X FACTOR** STAGE FOR THE FIRST OF THE LIVE SHOWS.

In **Week One** James started well, winning some **positive comments** from the judges, and survived the first public vote that saw **Carolynne** get evicted.

He came out fighting in **Week Two** with an emotional song, **No More Drama**, made famous by soul singer **Mary J Blige**. Just as importantly, James introduced his mentor, Nicole, to the charms of **pork scratchings** – a traditional British pub snack that looks like deep-fried wood shavings and tastes like... erm, deep-fried wood shavings.

AFTER HIS PERFORMANCE, THOUGH, JAMES SUFFERED AN ANXIETY ATTACK AND HAD TO RECEIVE URGENT MEDICAL ATTENTION. LUCKILY, HE RECOVERED QUICKLY AND WAS BACK ON STAGE ON SUNDAY EVENING TO HEAR HIS NAME CALLED FIRST – WHICH ALSO EASED HIS STRESS.

It was on to Week Three!

EVERY WEEK ON **THE X FACTOR**, THE
JUDGES GAVE THEIR VERDICT ON JAMES'S
PERFORMANCES. BUT CAN YOU MATCH UP THE
SONGS TO THE COMMENTS FROM THE JUDGES?

No More Drama

Sexy And I Know It

Sweet Dreams

Don't Speak

Hometown Glory

Let's Get It On

The Power Of Love

1. The **Tulisa** quote
'I felt like I was watching James Arthur at his own concert doing an album track. I loved it.'

⭐

2. The **Louis** quote
'Every week you bring something new to this show. You're a very dark, intense performer. That record deal can't be far away!'

⭐

3. The **Nicole** quote
'Every single word you breathe is just the truth, and I know you've made Mary J Blige proud tonight...'

⭐

4. The **Louis** quote
'What a great interpretation of the **LMFAO** song! When you get on that stage, you own it.'

⭐

5. The **Gary** quote
'What a vocal performance. Wow! I can't wait to buy your records.'

⭐

6. The **Nicole** quote
'That performance was genius, bellissimo, epic. It was transcendent! Beautiful.'

⭐

7. The **Gary** quote
'Adele is such an amazing, brilliant artist, no one should ever cover her songs – except for you! Your talent is absolutely incredible.'

45

All answers on pages 88-93

In **Week Three**, James sang the **LMFAO** song **Sexy And I Know It**, surrounded by dancers performing a specially choreographed routine. Eye-catching and successful – Gary told him it was the **PERFORMANCE OF THE SERIES**, and Dermot noticed that James must have enjoyed it because he 'nearly smiled'!

 What a serious young man!

Week Four was Hallowe'en, and James put on some scary guy-liner to perform a spooky version of Eurythmics's **Sweet Dreams**, surrounded by Grim Reapers, and hooded monks.

In the same week, James got to meet one of his heroes, **Robbie Williams**, who gave him some great advice and told him to be **true to himself**.

James marched on to Week Five.

I'm not going to lie – I have serenaded ladies I've been in love with before... It was my brilliant plan to get girls to like me! My guitar has seen me through lots of relationships and helped me get over heartbreak many times.

James Arthur

CAN YOU FEEL THE LOVE?

It's not just the public who love James – other performers do, too! Here are some of their thoughts about our James!

'I loved working with James week after week and seeing how he could take a song, turn it on its head and "James Arthur" it. He truly is an incredible artist and a real one-off and I am so excited to see what his future holds!'

Nicole Scherzinger

'I really like James Arthur... I'd love to get in the studio with him. I think he'd be great. He's brilliant.'

Emeli Sande

'From what I've heard from [James's debut album], it sounds amazing... His voice works on anything. I'm very sure he's gonna smash it and the record that we made, I'm sure it's gonna be massive... I'm very, very excited about this album.'

Labrinth, producer of James's debut album

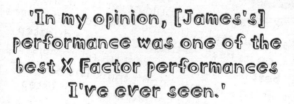

'In my opinion, [James's] performance was one of the best X Factor performances I've ever seen.'

Caroline Flack

In **WEEK FIVE** JAMES MET THE US BAND **NO DOUBT** AND PERFORMED ONE OF THEIR SONGS **DON'T SPEAK** ON THE LIVE SHOW. HE THOUGHT IT WAS DEFINITELY SCARIER PERFORMING THE SONG IN FRONT OF THE BAND, THAN IT WAS SINGING ON STAGE ON SATURDAY NIGHT!

In **Week Six** James tackled **Hometown Glory** by UK superstar singer **Adele**.

James is not afraid of a challenge!

'I'd always said I would never cover an **Adele** song unless I could find a way to turn it right on its head. In the end we put a **dubstep beat** behind it to make it sound completely fresh and new. I don't think **The X Factor** had ever had someone doing dubstep before!' **James Arthur**

Luckily it worked, and James was through to week seven!

X FACTOR boy band DISTRICT 3 and I used to have some good late night harmony sessions where we'd sing along to Chris Brown songs. Ella and I wrote a few tracks together as well and I would love to work with her one day. I could never do a duet with Jahmene, though. He would totally out-riff me!

James Arthur

JAMES'S X FACTOR JOURNEY
PART 2

FOR THE **10 WEEKS** OF **THE X FACTOR LIVE SHOWS**, OUR BOY DID A 'JAMES ARTHUR VERSION' OF AN EXISTING SONG TO MATCH EACH WEEK'S THEME!

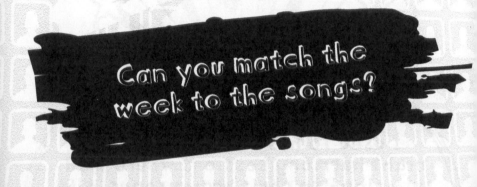

Can you match the week to the songs?

Week 6 Theme:
Best of British

Week 7 Theme:
Guilty Pleasures

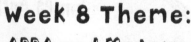

Week 8 Theme:
ABBA and Motown

Week 9 Theme:
Songs for you / Songs to get you to the final

Week 10 (Final: Part one) Theme:
Big Hits/Mentor Duets

Week 10 (Final: Part Two) Theme:
Song of the Series/Winner's single

Song choices

Impossible/Let's Get It On

One/The Power of Love

Feeling Good/Make You Feel My Love

Can't Take My Eyes Off You

Hometown Glory

SOS/Let's Get It On

53

All answers on pages 88-93

JAMES IS WELL KNOWN FOR HIS **BODY ART**, AND EVEN HAS **LOVE** AND **LIFE** TATTOOED ON HIS KNUCKLES.

One of his most recent tattoos is **namesake, King Arthur**, which James has had inked onto his right hand by celebrity tattooist Kevin Paul. Kevin, who has also provided tattoos for fellow popsters **Harry Styles**, **Ed Sheeran** and **Aston** from **JLS**, is helping James cover up some old amateur tattoos with some posher, smarter ones.

Which means LOTS of time under the needle for James. 'It has taken around 20 to 30 hours to do so far,' says Kevin. 'But I reckon it will take another 20 hours to finish.'

 Obviously James is not afraid of needles!

A GERMAN school teacher was such a James Arthur fan that she had a tattoo of his face on her leg!

James loves **TWITTER** – HE HAS NEARLY **2 MILLION FOLLOWERS** AND TWEETS NEARLY EVERY DAY. BUT CAN YOU GUESS WHICH OF THESE TWEETS ARE REAL AND WHICH ARE MADE UP?

1
@JamesArthur23
#NORTHEASTMUSIC

2
@JamesArthur23
Today is good

3
@JamesArthur23
Really fancy a curry and a night in #exhausted

4
@JamesArthur23
I'm tweeting on an aeroplane, I didn't think that was possible

5
@JamesArthur23
#getyourfeetoutforJA

⑥ @JamesArthur23
I JUST DO NOT LOSE AT FIFA!!!!

⑦ @JamesArthur23
Anchorman never gets old

⑧ @JamesArthur23
Can't wait for Alton Towers tomorrow!

⑨ @JamesArthur23
Belfast you were sick!! #LOVE

⑩ @JamesArthur23
Can't beat an episode of #CashInTheAttic #strangetastes

⑪ @JamesArthur23
Lost on my way to tonight's gig #doyouknowthewaytoSanJose?

⑫ @JamesArthur23
Open your eyes something beautiful is happening

57

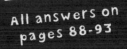
All answers on pages 88-93

THE COMPETITION WAS GETTING
TOUGHER AND TOUGHER, AND SOME
VERY TALENTED SINGERS WERE LEAVING
IN **WEEK SEVEN**, JAMES FOUND
HIMSELF IN THE BOTTOM TWO WITH
SINGER ELLA. AAARGH!

In the sing-off he performed **Alicia Keys' Fallin'** – the same song as his very first **X Factor** audition. Nicole and Gary voted to save him. Tulisa and Louis voted to save Ella. The **public voted** to keep James.

Phew, he was safe!

James had to bounce back quickly. Being in the **bottom two** made him determined to work harder than ever, and he wanted to give it everything!

Two great performances – including a version of **ABBA's SOS** and James was through to **Week Nine**. The Final was within touching distance!

If anyone had ever told me I would be singing an ABBA song on stage in front of millions of people one day, I would have laughed my head off. It was so far from anything I'd imagined myself doing.

James Arthur

Week Nine AND JAMES WAS ONE
STEP AWAY FROM THE FINAL. HE HAD
TO PREPARE FOR TWO OF THE MOST
IMPORTANT PERFORMANCES OF HIS LIFE!

Although he was no stranger to
singing in front of an audience, James
knew this was on another level.

**'With pub gigs you never know if
people are coming to see you or if
they just happen to be there having
a drink, so you don't really know if
they like you or not.'**

James's two songs that week were
a version of **U2's One** and **The
Power Of Love** by **Frankie Goes
To Hollywood**. Everything went
according to plan – no mistakes, just
pure emotion and the judges loved it!

**On the Sunday night, James
made it through to the Final
with Christopher and Jahmene.**

Hurrah!

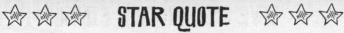

STAR QUOTE

I don't think I'd ever been
as nervous as I was on that
Sunday night. It was all down
to the public vote, so I was
praying they would support
me. When my name got called
out I just couldn't believe it.
I was beyond happy...
I was in the final!

James Arthur

THE WORLD CUP FINAL. THE WIMBLEDON FINAL. **THE X FACTOR FINAL.** THEY ALL HAVE ONE THING IN COMMON. THERE CAN ONLY BE ONE WINNER.

Making music costs money – recording studios, producers, marketing, music videos, the list goes on. But **The X Factor** winner gets all this for free. The chance to fulfill your lifetime's ambitions, and live the dream of becoming a real-life recording artist.

 Bring it On.

Jahmene and **Christopher** stood between James and the winner's podium. Was he going to let them get in his way? No, he wasn't!

On the Saturday night, the show went from three finalists down to two when Christopher was voted out. On the Sunday, James and Jahmene went head to head.

Just two more songs. James sang **Marvin Gaye's Let's Get It On** – one of his highlights from the series – and his winner's single **Impossible**. Both singers were brilliant, but our boy James was the nation's choice. **The X Factor winner 2012!**

'When Dermot read my name out, it didn't feel real at first. I was so stunned. The audience was screaming my name, and when I looked around I thought, 'I've actually done it – I've won THE X FACTOR.'

THE X FACTOR TOUR 2013

James and his fellow **X Factor finalists**
played 28 concerts in 13 cities over
34 action-packed days!

Manchester · Brighton · Cardiff
Nottingham · Liverpool · London
Birmingham · Newcastle · Sheffield
Glasgow · Aberdeen · Dublin
Belfast

James's song list included:

IMPOSSIBLE

SEXY AND I KNOW IT

LET'S GET IT ON

THE POWER OF LOVE

Did you see the show?

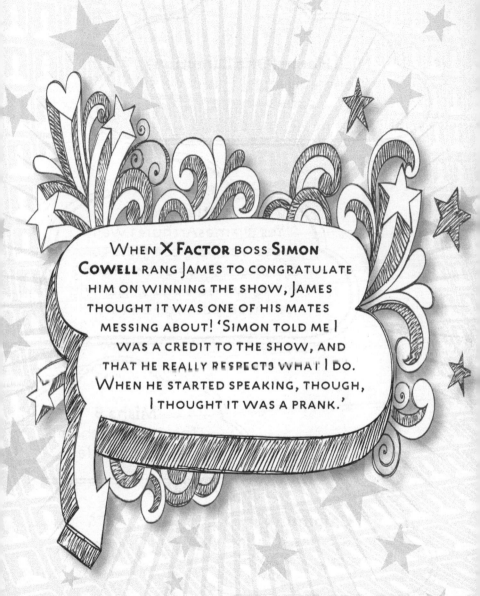

When **X Factor** boss **Simon Cowell** rang James to congratulate him on winning the show, James thought it was one of his mates messing about! 'Simon told me I was a credit to the show, and that he really respects what I do. When he started speaking, though, I thought it was a prank.'

Niall Horan (One Direction)
'Congrats James! This dude is gone be huge.'

Little Mix
'Yes @JamesArthur23 well deserved!! Big congrats to @JahmeneDouglas two both worthy winners and amazingly talented lads...roll on 2013!'

Misha B
'The people's champ takes the title!'

Chipmunk
'Sick @JamesArthur23 ima buy ur album'

Cheryl Cole
'Congratulations James Arthur, true talent!'

Holly Willoughby
'James Arthur all the way'

Tinchy Stryder
'James Arthur did an **Adele** song, one of my faves & killed it, not many people can do that!!... He's gonna go so far man!! #Salute

Professor Green
'James Arthur sounded wicked singing **Hometown Glory**.'

CELEBRITY GIRLFRIENDS

THE NEWSPAPERS LIKE TO LINK JAMES
TO EVERY FAMOUS CELEBRITY FEMALE
HE MEETS. SO WHO **HASN'T** JAMES BEEN
LINKED TO IN THE PRESS?

Rita Ora
Spotted at an **X Factor** Live after party with the **Shine Ya Light** singer.

Danielle Peazer
Met Liam Payne's (**One Direction**) ex-girlfriend on **The X Factor** tour.

Kimberley Garner
Had dinner with the **Made In Chelsea** star at London restaurant Hakkasan.

Caroline Flack
James admits to asking the **Xtra Factor** presenter out SIX times. She says he has 'beautiful eyes'.

Taylor Swift
The pair were seen together at the **British Grand Prix.**

Rihanna
James met Rihanna at a party hosted by **Jay-Z** in London during recent live shows.

All answers on pages 88-93

68

James on a night out with reality TV star Kimberley Garner.

 # SUPERFAN NAMES

JUSTIN BEIBER HAS HIS BELIEBERS.
ONE DIRECTION HAVE THEIR
DIRECTIONERS. SO WHAT DOES
JAMES WANT HIS FANS TO BE CALLED?

The Knights of
the Round Table

James A Knights

Super JAs

The James Gang

The Arthurians

All answers on pages 88-93

CANADIAN-BORN DANCER LUKAS
MCFARLANE WON SKY ONE SHOW **GOT
TO DANCE 2013** BY PERFORMING TO
JAMES'S WINNER'S SINGLE **IMPOSSIBLE**!
LUKAS SAYS:

'When James sings, it's the way I feel when I dance, and I would love to collaborate with him on anything because I just think he is such a true artist. Hearing him makes me want to move.'

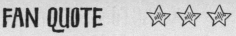

What I like best about James is that he makes you feel something special in every song he sings. He's so great at putting emotion into his voice. He gives me goosebumps whenever I listen to him!

Seren, 14

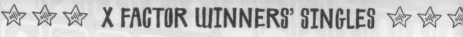

IF YOU'RE A POP FAN WITH A NOSE FOR TRIVIA, YOU'LL ALREADY KNOW THAT JAMES'S WINNER'S SINGLE **IMPOSSIBLE** WAS A COVER VERSION. BUT WHO SANG THE ORIGINAL? AND WHO SANG THE ORIGINAL OF PREVIOUS WINNERS' SINGLES?

2012

James Arthur

IMPOSSIBLE

2011

Little Mix

CANNONBALL

2010

Matt Cardle

WHEN WE COLLIDE

2009

Joe McElderry

THE CLIMB

2008

Alexandra Burke

HALLELUJAH

Who were the original recording artists of which songs?!

Leonard Cohen
★
Biffy Clyro
★
Miley Cyrus
★
Shontelle
★
Damien Rice

75

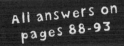
All answers on pages 88-93

James's **X Factor** single was loved by fans, selling a million copies in a month, and earning a BRIT nomination for Best British Single. Here are some examples of what the critics thought...

'The raw talent and gritty vocals [James] possesses manage to shine perfectly throughout the song, improving on the original by miles and showing exactly why he took the crown as X FACTOR 2012 champion'.

'**Impossible** succeeds best in the raw pain of James Arthur's voice. Modulating somewhere between winter blues and being devastatingly broken, his gravelly timbre helps to lift a middling R&B track into something with more substance.'

'The lyrics are strong and the chorus has great catchiness and singability.'

'A classic tale of heartbreak but with the weighty vocal from James it's transformed into a story full of pain and determination summing up his story perfectly. Thanks to his guttural vocals in the song's final minute, James manages to make the song his own and hit you with some emotion'.

IF YOU WANT TO BE A POP STAR, IT
HELPS TO HAVE A RECOGNISABLE LOOK.
OUR BOY JAMES HAS A SIMPLE BUT
STRONG WARDROBE THAT SHOUTS

>>> COOL! <<<

Here's how he does it:

Shirt with top button done up
(very important!)

skinny dark jeans

Hi-top trainers or leather boots

Fitted suit jackets (sometimes
with sleeves rolled up)

stubbly beard

Denim jacket

 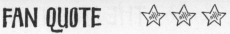

James gave **THE X FACTOR** something that it lacked. **NOT** just a super-talented singer but someone with heart and soul. Someone who had been through hard times, and could express that pain whenever they sang. It helps that he is super cute too!

Caroline, 15

OK, SO HERE IS YOUR CHANCE TO PROVE THAT YOU'RE A JAMES ARTHUR SUPERFAN. CONCENTRATE NOW! GRAB A PIECE OF PAPER AND A PEN TO WRITE DOWN YOUR ANSWERS. WE'RE EXPECTING YOU TO PASS THIS WITH FLYING COLOURS...

1.

In what year was James born?

a) 1991
b) 1990
c) 1989
d) 1988

2.

What is James's middle name?

a) Andrew
b) Adam
c) Anthony
d) Arthur

3.

What are the names of James's mum and dad?

a) Shirley and Neil
b) Margaret and Alan
c) Jane and James
d) June and Trevor

4.

How many brothers and sisters does James have?

a) None, he's an only child
b) One brother, three sisters
c) Two brothers, two sisters
d) Three brothers, one sister

5.

What star sign is James?

a) Capricorn
b) Pisces
c) Aquarius
d) Cancer

81

All answers on pages 88-93

1.

What sign of the Chinese Zodiac was James born in?

a) Year of the Rabbit
b) Year of the Goat
c) Year of the Dragon
d) Year of the Rooster

2.

In what Middle Eastern country did James live?

a) Dubai
b) Qatar
c) UAE
d) Bahrain

3.

What song did James sing at his very first X Factor audition?

a) **Rule The World** by Take That
b) **Hot Legs** by Rod Stewart
c) **Fallin'** by Alicia Keys
d) **Diamonds** by Rihanna

4.

What city did James visit for Judges' Houses?

a) Dubai
b) Las Vegas
c) Los Angeles
d) London

5.

Which Adele song did James cover in The X Factor Week Six?

a) Skyfall
b) Someone Like You
c) Hometown Glory
d) Rolling In The Deep

6.

Which ABBA song did James cover in The X Factor Week Eight?

a) Dancing Queen
b) Mamma Mia
c) SOS
d) The Winner Takes It All

1.

Which contestant did James beat in The X Factor Final?

a) Christopher Maloney
b) Jahmene Douglas
c) Rylan Clark
d) Ella Henderson

2.

Who sang the original version of James's winner's single Impossible?

a) Shontelle
b) Beyonce
c) Alexandra Burke
d) Leona Lewis

3.

How many copes did 'Impossible' sell in the first 24 hours of release?

a) 53,000
b) 94,000
c) 144,000
d) 187,000

4.

How many weeks did 'Impossible' spend at UK Number One?

a) One
b) Two
c) Three
d) Four

5.

Which producer is James working with on their debut album?

a) Daft Punk
b) Kanye West
c) Labrinth
d) Calvin Harris

6.

Which reality TV star has James been spotted having dinner with?

a) Kimberley Garner, **Made In Chelsea**
b) Sam Faiers, **The Only Way Is Essex**
c) Millie Mackintosh, **Made In Chelsea**
d) Billie Faiers, **The Only Way Is Essex**

All answers on pages 88-93

Winning **The X Factor** is only the start of James's journey to superstardom. In August 2013 he announced the title of his new single **You're Nobody 'Til Somebody Loves You** ahead of his debut album. But what else do you think will happen to him over the next five years?

James breaks America, and celebrates a Number One single and a Number One album over there. He performs at half-time at the Superbowl.

James has three back-to-back triple-platinum albums, and becomes Britain's most successful recording artist of the decade.

James records one album then retires from music to run a B&B back home.

James marries Rita Ora and they become a double act called The Orthurs.

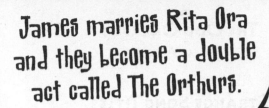

James joins **The Xtra Factor** for the next series of **The X Factor**, interviewing contestants back stage, and generally being a cheeky chap like Olly Murs.

James collaborates with Professor Green on a single. They both dress as each other and fans have to guess which one is which!

James replaces Louis Walsh as a judge on the next series of **The X Factor**.

JAMES RELEASES A NEW SINGLE THAT EVERYONE LOVES. HE RETURNS TO **THE X FACTOR** TO PERFORM IT AND GETS A HERO'S WELCOME.

P22
The Odd One Out
Home Alone

P23
Strange Song Titles
Real songs
Skinny Chimp
Misguided Beard
Juliet is Not Dead
Hole in My Heart
Tonight We Dine in Hades
Superhero

Made up songs
Lost a Fiver
Drastic Action
Fatal Mistake
Hero Worship

P34-35
Judges' House
Louis Walsh 2012
Las Vegas

Nicole Scherzinger 2012
Dubai

Tulisa 2012
St Lucia

Gary Barlow 2012
London

Louis Walsh 2011
Barcelona

Tulisa 2011
Greece

Gary Barlow 2011
Los Angeles

Kelly Rowland 2011
Miami

Louis Walsh 2010
Shannon, Republic of Ireland

Dannii Minogue 2010
Melbourne

Cheryl Cole 2010
Los Angeles

Simon Cowell 2010
Spain

P40-41
James's X Factor Journey Part 1

Week 1
Theme: Heroes
Song choice: Stronger

Week 2
Theme: Love and heartbreak
Song choice: No More Drama

Week 3
Theme: Club classics
Song choice: Sexy And I Know It

Week 4
Theme: Hallowe'en
Song choice: Sweet Dreams (Are Made Of This)

Week 5
Theme: Numbers Ones
Song choice: Don't Speak

QUIZ QUESTIONS ANSWERS

P44-45
THEY SAID WHAT?

NO MORE DRAMA
3. NICOLE

SEXY AND I KNOW IT
4. LOUIS

SWEET DREAMS
2. LOUIS

DON'T SPEAK
1. TULISA

HOMETOWN GLORY
7. GARY

LET'S GET IT ON
5. GARY

THE POWER OF LOVE
6. NICOLE

P52-53
JAMES'S X FACTOR JOURNEY PART 2

WEEK 6
THEME: BEST OF BRITISH
SONG CHOICE: **HOMETOWN GLORY**

WEEK 7
THEME: GUILTY PLEASURES
SONG CHOICE: **CAN'T TAKE MY EYES OFF YOU**

WEEK 8
THEME: ABBA AND MOTOWN
SONG CHOICE: **SOS/LET'S GET IT ON**

WEEK 9
THEME: SONGS FOR YOU/SONGS TO GET YOU TO THE FINAL
SONG CHOICE: **ONE/THE POWER OF LOVE**

WEEK 10 (THE FINAL PART ONE)
THEME: BIG HITS/MENTOR DUETS
SONG CHOICE: **FEELING GOOD/MAKE YOU FEEL MY LOVE**

WEEK 10 (THE FINAL PART TWO)
THEME: SONG OF THE SERIES/WINNER'S SINGLE
SONG CHOICE: **LET'S GET IT ON/IMPOSSIBLE**

P56-57

A TWIT OF A GENIUS

TRUE
1, 2, 4, 5, 6, 7, 9, 12

FALSE
3, 8, 10, 11

P68

CELEBRITY GIRLFRIENDS

RITA ORA
TRUE

DANIELLE PEAZER
TRUE

KIMBERLEY GARNER
TRUE

CAROLINE FLACK
TRUE

TAYLOR SWIFT
FALSE

RIHANNA
FALSE

P70
SUPERFAN NAMES

a) THE KNIGHTS OF THE ROUND TABLE

P74-75
X FACTOR WINNERS' SINGLES

2012
IMPOSSIBLE
ORIGINALLY RECORDED BY SHONTELLE

2011
CANNONBALL
ORIGINALLY RECORDED BY DAMIEN RICE

2010
WHEN WE COLLIDE
ORIGINALLY RECORDED BY BIFFY CLYRO

2009
THE CLIMB
ORIGINALLY RECORDED BY MILEY CYRUS

2008
HALLELUJAH
ORIGINALLY RECORDED BY LEONARD COHEN

P80-81
THE BIG QUIZ PART I

1. D) 1988

2. A) ANDREW

3. A) SHIRLEY AND NEIL

4. B) ONE BROTHER, THREE SISTERS

5. B) PISCES

P82-83
THE BIG QUIZ PART II

1. C) YEAR OF THE DRAGON

2. D) BAHRAIN

3. C) FALLIN' BY ALICIA KEYS

4. A) DUBAI

5. C) HOMETOWN GLORY

6. C) SOS

P84-85
THE BIG QUIZ PART III

1. B) JAHMENE DOUGLAS

2. A) SHONTELLE

3. D) 187,000

4. B) TWO

5. C) LABRINTH

6. A) KIMBERLEY GARNER, MADE IN CHELSEA

Congratulations!

Now you really, truly **KNOW** your idol
(probably better than his own mum). But
what about your **OTHER** idols, like
One Direction, **Justin Bieber**, **Katy Perry**,
Robert Pattinson and **Olly Murs?**

WHAT ABOUT THEM...?

DON'T PANIC.

Simply check out the other titles
in the series and become an

EVEN
BIGGER
FAN.

95

Want to Know Your Idol?

TOTALLY AWESOME TITLES IN THE SERIES:

9780750279321

9780750279338

9780750279307

9780750279314

9780750278386

9780750278362

WHY NOT COLLECT THEM ALL?